The Call of the Divine Beloved

Selected Mystical Works of Bahá'u'lláh

The Call of the Divine Beloved

Selected Mystical Works of Bahá'u'lláh

Bahá'í World Centre

Haifa

CONTENTS

v

"At one time We spoke in the language of the lawgiver", Bahá'u'lláh writes in the Epistle to the Son of the Wolf, "at another in that of the truth-seeker and the mystic".[1] The present volume brings together a selection of His Tablets which were revealed in the language of the mystic. Some are widely known; others are published here for the first time in English translation.

Although most of the Tablets in this collection were revealed during Bahá'u'lláh's sojourn in 'Iráq (1853–1863), the first, the poem known as "Rashḥ-i-'Amá", was written in 1852 in the Síyáh-Chál and is among the few He revealed while in His native land of Persia, and in verse. Bahá'u'lláh recounts: "During the days I lay in the prison of Ṭihrán, though the galling weight of the chains and the stench-filled air allowed Me but little sleep, still in those infrequent moments of slumber I felt as if something flowed from the crown of My head over My breast, even as a mighty torrent that precipitateth itself upon the earth from the summit of a lofty mountain. Every limb of My body would, as a result, be set afire. At such moments My tongue recited what no man could bear to hear."[2] The poetic reflection of that experience, as conveyed in Rashḥ-i-'Amá, can perhaps never be adequately rendered into another language, yet the present translation is an initial attempt to impart a glimpse of its power and momentous themes.

In 'Iráq, during the two years Bahá'u'lláh sought seclusion in the mountains of Kurdistán, far from the malice and dissension that had blighted the Bábí community in Baghdád, word of His presence in Sulaymáníyyih attracted religious scholars and mystics of the region, including several prominent Ṣúfí shaykhs, to seek out the One Who dwelt as a humble dervish yet evinced a wisdom that was profound and a power of expression unequalled: "Through His numerous discourses and epistles", Shoghi Effendi writes, "He disclosed new vistas to their eyes, resolved the perplexities that agitated their minds, unfolded the inner meaning of many hitherto obscure passages in the writings of various commentators, poets and theologians … 'In a short time,' is 'Abdu'l-Bahá's own testimony, 'Kurdistán was magnetized with His love. During this period Bahá'u'lláh lived in poverty. His garments were those of the poor and needy. His food was that of the indigent and lowly. An atmosphere of majesty haloed Him as the sun at midday. Everywhere He was greatly revered and loved.'"[3]

When Bahá'u'lláh returned to Baghdád, His Kurdish admirers followed. The sight of 'ulamá and Ṣúfí shaykhs flocking to visit Bahá'u'lláh astonished the religious leaders of the city, who also began to seek His presence—and became enthralled. Their esteem for Him in turn attracted others, from poets and mystics to government officials, and further spread His fame.

This period, Shoghi Effendi tells us, saw an "enormous expansion in the scope and volume of Bahá'u'lláh's writings … The verses that streamed during those years from His pen, described as 'a copious rain' by Himself, whether in the form of epistles, exhortations, commentaries, apologies, dissertations, prophecies, prayers, odes or specific Tablets" revivified and transformed the Bábí community. It was a period so prolific that, on average, the unrecorded verses He would reveal in a single day and night equalled in number those of the Qur'án. "As to those verses which He either dictated or wrote Himself, their number was no less remarkable than either the wealth of material they contained, or the diversity of subjects to which they referred."[4]

Among the "priceless treasures cast forth from the billowing ocean of Bahá'u'lláh's Revelation" in those days is Bahá'u'lláh's "greatest mystical composition", the Seven Valleys, which "describes the seven stages which the soul of the seeker must needs traverse ere it can attain the object of its existence."[5] Writing years later in 'Akká, He explained:

This treatise was revealed in the language of the people, in the days prior to Our Declaration. The occasion for its revelation was the receipt of a letter addressed to the Most Holy Court in 'Iráq from a man of Sunní persuasion, who was both a scholar and a mystic. This treatise was therefore revealed, in accordance with divine wisdom, in the manner that was current amongst the people. However, in this day, every soul

who hath fixed his gaze upon the Supreme
Horizon, and hath recognized the one true
God, hath verily attained unto every one
of the seven valleys or seven stations mentioned therein.[6]

Like the twelfth-century poem by 'Aṭṭár,
Manṭiqu'ṭ-Ṭayr (*The Conference of the Birds*), the
Seven Valleys describes a journey through seven
stations in quest of the Divine. However, the quest
in the Seven Valleys is also one undertaken in a
context defined by the imminent dawning of the
new Revelation—and indeed the presence of the
Beloved Himself.

That the mystic journey cannot be reduced
to a fixed scheme, nor the search for the Divine
Beloved to a series of discrete stages, is highlighted
in a number of other Tablets, four of which are
included here. The volume closes with the Four
Valleys, an epistle addressed to one of Bahá'u'lláh's
devoted admirers from Kurdistán. Rather than
describing a progression through stages, it elabo-
rates four different paths of approach to the
Divine.

The current renderings of the Seven Valleys
and the Four Valleys are based on the translations

by Marzieh Gail, in consultation with Ali-Kuli Khan, published in 1945. While those earlier translations contain many exquisite, inspired passages, some changes were required for clarity and accuracy.

May the publication of this volume contribute to a deeper appreciation of the mystical dimensions of Bahá'u'lláh's Message and inspire a greater zeal and fervour in raising the celestial call of the Divine Beloved: "For whereas in days past every lover besought and searched after his Beloved, it is the Beloved Himself Who now is calling His lovers and is inviting them to attain His presence."[7]

I

Ra<u>sh</u>ḥ-i-'Amá
(The Clouds of the Realms Above)

'TIS FROM Our rapture that the clouds of   1
   realms above are raining down;[8]
'Tis from Our anthem that the mysteries of faith
   are raining down.

Upon the Eastern wind Cathay's entrancing musk   2
   doth waft;
This sweetly scented breeze from Our curling
   locks is raining down.

The day-star of adornment hath dawned forth   3
   above the face of God;
Behold that mystic truth which from His
   Countenance is raining down.

The sea of purity hath from the wave of true   4
   reunion surged;
This precious, rare bestowal from our rapture
   is raining down.

5   The treasuries of love lay hid within the very
      heart of Fárs;
   From out this treasure trove the pearls of
      faithfulness are raining down.

6   The splendour of the rose doth bring the ecstasy
      of choicest wine;
   This subtle music from the ringing tones of
      Lordship is raining down.

7   The trumpet-blast of Judgement Day, the joyful
      bliss of heaven's call—
   Both at a single breath are from the firmament
      now raining down.

8   The Day of "I am He" is made to shine resplendent
      from Our face;
   The Age of "He is He" from out Our flowing cup
      is raining down.

9   From out the fountain of Our heart hath God's
      celestial river flowed;
   This cup of honeyed nectar from Our ruby lips
      is raining down.

The Day of God hath been fulfilled, for lo, the 10
    Lord hath been unveiled;
This wondrous message from the melody of Ṭá'
    is raining down.

Behold Bahá's outpouring grace, the bounty of 11
    the clouds above,
Which, merged into a single song, in God's own
    voice is raining down.

Behold the Lord's leviathan, behold His sacred 12
    countenance;
Behold the blessings of the heart that from His
    throne are raining down.

Behold the Palm of Paradise, behold the warbling 13
    of the Dove;
Behold the glorious hymns that in the purest light
    are raining down.

Behold the soul-entrancing song, behold the 14
    beating of the drum,
Behold the sacred rhythms that from Our
    hand are raining down.

15   Behold the Countenance Divine! Behold the
      Maid of Paradise!
  Behold the grace upon the world from Our own
      presence raining down.

16   Behold the everlasting Face! Behold the chalice-
      bearer's charm!
  Behold the crystal draught that from Our
      brimming cup is raining down.

17   Behold the fire of Moses, see His hand that
      shineth white;
  Behold the heart of Sinai—from Our hand all
      raining down.

18   Hear ye the sotted lovers' sighs, behold the garden
      blooming fair;
  Behold the bliss that from His presence in your
      midst is raining down.

19   Behold the radiant face of Há', behold the
      beauteous robe of Bá';
  Behold the Lordly grace that from Our Pen is
      raining down.

The vessel of the Advent this, the clouds of   20
  limpid waters these;
The trill of songbirds this, from Our fleeting
  Wellspring raining down.

2

The Seven Valleys

*An exposition of the mysteries
enshrined in the stages of ascent for
them that seek to journey unto God,
the Almighty, the Ever-Forgiving*

IN THE NAME OF GOD, THE MERCIFUL,
THE COMPASSIONATE!

PRAISE BE to God Who hath made being to come forth from nothingness; graven upon the tablet of man a measure of the mysteries of His eternity; taught him from the storehouse of divine utterance that which he knew not; made him a perspicuous book unto such as have believed and surrendered their souls; given him to behold, in this dark and ruinous age, a new creation within all things; and caused him to speak forth, from the midmost heart of eternity, and in a new and wondrous voice, embodied in the most excellent Temple.⁹ And all to this end: that every man may testify, in himself and by himself, before the Seat of the revelation of his Lord, that there is none other God but Him; and that all may reach that summit of realities where none shall contemplate anything but that he shall perceive God therein. This is the vision of the splendours which have been deposited within the realities of all things; for otherwise He, exalted be His glory, is entirely sanctified above being seen or witnessed: "No vision taketh in Him, but He taketh in all vision; He is the Subtile, the All-Perceiving."[10]

2   And I praise and glorify that primal Sea which hath branched out from the ocean of the unseen Essence, and that primal Morn which hath broken forth upon the horizon of Singleness, and that primal Sun which hath risen in the heaven of everlasting splendour, and that primal Fire which was kindled from the Lamp of eternity within the Niche of oneness: He Who is called "Aḥmad" in the kingdom of the exalted ones, and "Muḥammad" amongst the concourse of the favoured ones, and "Maḥmúd" in the realm of the sincere;[11] and in the hearts of the knowing, "whichsoever ye call upon, most beauteous are His names."[12] And upon His kindred

and His companions be abundant, abiding, and eternal peace!

To continue: I have hearkened to the song of the nightingale of knowledge upon the twigs of the tree of thine inmost being, and to the cooing of the dove of certitude upon the branches of the bower of thine heart. Methinks I inhaled the fragrance of purity from the raiment of thy love and, in perusing thy letter, attained thy very presence. I noted, moreover, thine allusions to thy death in God and thy life through Him, and the love thou dost cherish for the beloved of the Lord and for the Manifestations of His names and the Exponents of His attributes. I have purposed, therefore, to acquaint thee with holy and resplendent tokens from the realms of might and glory, that haply they may draw thee nigh unto the court of holiness, nearness, and beauty, and draw thee to a station wherein thou shalt see naught in all existence but the hallowed Countenance of thy Beloved, and wilt behold all of creation as a day wherein none was deemed worthy of mention.[13]

Of this did the nightingale of oneness sing in the garden of his mystical treatise,[14] saying, "And there shall appear upon the tablet of thine heart an inscription of the subtle mysteries of the verse 'Fear ye God; God will teach you', and the bird of thy spirit shall recall the sanctuaries of ancient splendour, and soar upon the wings of longing into the heaven of the command 'Walk the beaten paths of thy Lord', and partake of the choice fruits of communion in the gardens of the utterance 'Feed, moreover, on every kind of fruit.'"[15]

5   By My life, O friend! Wert thou to taste the fruits of these verdant trees that spring from the soil of true understanding, once the effulgent light of His Essence hath been reflected in the Mirrors of His names and attributes yearning would seize the reins of patience and restraint from out thy hand and stir thy spirit into commotion with the splendours of His light. It would draw thee from this abode of dust unto thy true and heavenly habitation in the midmost heart of mystic knowledge, and raise thee to a station wherein thou wilt soar in the air even as thou treadest upon the earth, and wilt walk upon the water even as thou movest over the land. Wherefore, may it rejoice me, and thee, and whosoever mounteth into the heaven of knowledge, and whose heart hath been revived by the breezes of certitude that waft from the Sheba of the All-Merciful upon the

meadow of his inner being. Peace be upon him who followeth the way of guidance![16]

And further: the stages that mark the wayfarers' journey from their mortal abode to the heavenly homeland are said to be seven. Some have referred to them as seven valleys, and others, as seven cities.[17] And it is said that until the wayfarer taketh leave of self and traverseth these stages, he shall never attain the ocean of nearness and reunion nor taste of the matchless wine. 6

The first is THE VALLEY OF SEARCH. The steed of this valley is patience; without patience the wayfarer on this journey will reach nowhere and attain no goal. Nor should he ever become downhearted: If he strive for a hundred thousand years and yet fail to behold the beauty of the Friend, he should not falter. For those who seek the Kaaba of "for Us" rejoice in the tidings "In Our ways shall We assuredly guide them."[18] In their search, they have stoutly girded up the loins of service and at every moment journey from the plane of heedlessness into the realm of search. No bond shall hold them back and no counsel deter them. 7

It is incumbent upon these servants to cleanse the heart, which is the wellspring of divine 8 treasures, of every marking; turn away from imitation, which is following the traces of their forefathers; and shut the door of friendship and enmity upon all the people of the earth.

9   In this journey the seeker reacheth a station wherein he seeth all created things wandering distracted in search of the Friend. How many a Jacob will he see searching after his Joseph, how many a lover will he behold hastening towards the Well-Beloved; a world of adoring souls will he witness tracing the path of the Adored One! At every moment he findeth a weighty matter, in every hour he becometh aware of a new mystery; for he hath severed his heart from both worlds and set out for the Kaaba of the Beloved. At every step, aid from the invisible Realm will attend him and the fervour of his search will grow.

10   One must judge of search by the standard of the Majnún of love.[19] It is related that one day they came upon Majnún sifting the dust, his tears flowing down. They asked, "What doest thou?" He said, "I seek for Laylí." "Alas for thee!" they cried, "Laylí is of pure spirit, yet thou seekest her in the dust!" He said, "I seek her everywhere; haply somewhere I shall find her."

11   Yea, though to the wise it be shameful to seek

the Lord of Lords in the dust, yet this betokeneth intense ardour in searching. "Whoso seeketh out a thing and persisteth with zeal shall find it."[20]

The true seeker hunteth naught but the object [12] of his quest, and the sincere lover hath no desire save reunion with his beloved. Nor shall the seeker reach his goal unless he sacrifice all things. That is, whatever he hath seen, and heard, and understood—all he must set at naught with "no God is there", that he may enter into the realm of the spirit, which is the city of "but God".[21] Labour is needed, if we are to seek Him; ardour is needed, if we are to drink the nectar of reunion with Him; and if we taste of this cup, we shall cast away the world.

On this journey the wayfarer dwelleth in [13] every abode, however humble, and resideth in every land. In every face he seeketh the beauty of the Friend; in every region he searcheth after the Beloved. He joineth every company and seeketh fellowship with every soul, that haply in some heart he may discern the secret of the Beloved, or in some face behold the beauty of the Adored One.

And if, by the help of the Creator, he findeth [14] on this journey a trace of the traceless Friend,

and inhaleth the fragrance of the long-lost Joseph
from the heavenly herald, he shall straightway step
into THE VALLEY OF LOVE and be consumed in the
fire of love. In this city the heaven of rapture is
upraised, and the world-illuming sun of yearning
shineth, and the fire of love is set ablaze; and when
the fire of love is ablaze, it burneth to ashes the
harvest of reason.

15   Now is the wayfarer oblivious of himself, and
of aught besides himself. He seeth neither ignorance nor knowledge, neither doubt nor certitude;
he knoweth not the morn of guidance from the
night of error. He fleeth from both unbelief and
faith, and findeth in deadly poison his heart's
relief. Wherefore 'Aṭṭár saith:

> For the infidel, error—for the faithful, faith;
> For 'Aṭṭár's heart, an atom of thy pain.

16   The steed of this valley is pain, and if there
be no pain this journey will never end. In this
plane the lover hath no thought save the Beloved,
and seeketh no refuge save the Friend. At every
moment he offereth a hundred lives in the path
of the Loved One, at every step he throweth a
thousand heads at His feet.

O My brother! Until thou enter the Egypt of 17
love, thou shalt never gaze upon the Joseph-like
beauty of the Friend; and until, like Jacob, thou
forsake thine outward eyes, thou shalt never open
the eye of thine inward being; and until thou burn
with the fire of love, thou shalt never find thyself
in the true yearning's embrace.

A lover feareth nothing and can suffer no harm: 18
Thou seest him chill in the fire and dry in the sea.

A lover is he who is chill in hellfire;
A knower is he who is dry in the sea.[22]

Love accepteth no existence and wisheth no 19
life: In death it seeth life, and in shame it seeketh
glory. To merit the madness of love, one must
abound in sanity; to merit the bonds of the Friend,
one must be free in spirit. Blessed the neck
that is caught in His noose, and happy the head
that falleth on the dust in the path of His love.
Wherefore, O friend, renounce thy self, that thou
mayest find the Peerless One; and soar beyond
this mortal world, that thou mayest find thy nest
in the abode of heaven. Be as naught, if thou
wouldst kindle the fire of being and be fit for the
pathway of love.

> Ne'er will love allow a living soul to tread
>   its way;
> Ne'er will the falcon deign to seize a lifeless
>   prey.[23]

20   Love setteth a world aflame at every turn and layeth waste every land wherein it raiseth its banner. Being hath no existence in its kingdom; the wise wield no command within its realm. The leviathan of love swalloweth the master of reason and slayeth the lord of knowledge. It drinketh the seven seas, but its heart's thirst is still unquenched and it asketh, "Is there yet any more?"[24] It shunneth its own self and draweth away from all on earth.

> Love's a stranger to earth and heaven too;
> In him are lunacies seventy and two.[25]

21   Love hath bound a myriad victims in its fetters and pierced a myriad wise men with its arrow. Know that every redness thou seest in the world is from its wrath, and every paleness in men's cheeks is from its poison. It yieldeth no remedy but death and walketh not save in the valley of extinction; yet sweeter than honey is its venom upon the

lover's lips, and fairer its deadly sting, in the seeker's sight, than a hundred thousand lives.

Wherefore must the veils of the satanic self [22] be burned away in the fire of love, that the spirit may be cleansed and refined, and thus may apprehend the station of Him but for Whom the world would not have been created.[26]

> Kindle the fire of love and burn away
>   all things;
> Then set thy foot into the land of the
>   lovers.[27]

And if, confirmed by the Creator, the lover [23] escapeth the claws of the eagle of love, he will enter THE REALM OF KNOWLEDGE and come out of doubt into certitude, and turn from the darkness of wayward desire to the guiding light of the fear of God. His inner eye will open and he will privily converse with his Beloved; he will unlock the gates of truth and supplication and shut the doors of idle fancy. He in this realm is content with the divine decree, and seeth war as peace, and in death findeth the meaning of everlasting life. With both inward and outward eyes he witnesseth the mysteries of resurrection in the realms of creation and in the souls of men, and with a spiritual heart apprehendeth the wisdom of God in His endless manifestations. In the sea he findeth a drop, in a drop he beholdeth the secrets of the sea.

> Split the atom's heart, and lo!
> Within it thou wilt find a sun.[28]

24   Gazing with the eye of absolute insight, the wayfarer in this valley seeth in God's creation neither contradiction nor incongruity, and at every moment exclaimeth, "No defect canst thou see in the creation of the God of mercy. Repeat the gaze: Seest thou a single flaw?"[29] He beholdeth justice in injustice, and in justice, grace. In ignorance he findeth many a knowledge hidden, and in knowledge a myriad wisdoms manifest. He breaketh the cage of the body and the hold of the passions, and communeth with the denizens of the immortal realm. He scaleth the ladders of inner truth and hasteneth to the heaven of inner meanings. He rideth in the ark of "We will surely show them Our signs in the world and within themselves", and saileth upon the sea of "until it become plain to them that it is the truth".[30]

And if he meeteth with injustice he shall have patience, and if he cometh upon wrath he shall manifest love.

There was once a lover, it is said, who had [25] sighed for long years in separation from his beloved, and wasted in the fire of remoteness. From the rule of love, his breast was void of patience and his body weary of his spirit; he reckoned life without her as a mockery, and the world consumed him away. How many a day he found no respite from his longing; how many a night the pain of her kept him from sleep. His body was worn to a sigh, and his heart's wound had turned him to a cry of sorrow. A thousand lives would he freely have given for one taste of the cup of her presence, and yet even this was not within his reach. The doctors knew no cure for him, and companions avoided his company; yea, physicians have no remedy for one sick of love, unless the favour of the beloved deliver him.

At last the tree of his longing yielded the fruit [26] of despair, and the fire of his hope fell to ashes. Then one night he could bear life no more, and he left his house for the marketplace. On a sudden, a watchman followed after him. He broke into a run, with the watchman in swift pursuit; then other watchmen came together and barred every passage to the weary one. And that wretched one cried from his heart, and ran here and there, and moaned to himself, "Surely this watchman is 'Izrá'íl, my angel of death, following so fast upon me, or he is a tyrant of men, prompted by hatred and malice." His feet carried him on—that hapless one bleeding with the arrow of love—while his heart lamented. Then he came to a garden wall, and with untold pain and trouble he scaled it. He saw that it was very high; yet, forgetting his life, he threw himself down into the garden.

27   And there he beheld his beloved with a lamp in her hand, searching for a ring she had lost. When the heart-surrendered lover looked upon his ravishing love, he drew a great breath and lifted his hands in prayer, crying, "O God! Bestow honour upon the watchman, and riches and long life. For the watchman was Gabriel, guiding this poor one; or he was Isráfíl, bringing life to this wretched one!"

28   Indeed, his words were true; for he had found many a secret justice in this seeming tyranny of the watchman, and had seen how many a mercy lay hid behind the veil. In one stroke of wrath, the guard had joined one who was athirst in the desert

of love to the sea of the beloved, and dispelled the darkness of separation with the shining light of reunion. He had led one who was afar to the garden of nearness, and guided an ailing soul to the heart's physician.

Now if the lover could have seen the end, he would from the beginning have blessed the watchman, prayed God on his behalf, and seen his tyranny as justice; but since the end was veiled to him, he lamented and made his plaint in the beginning. Yet those who journey in the garden land of true knowledge, since they see the end in the beginning, behold peace in war and conciliation in enmity. [29]

Such is the state of the wayfarers in this valley, but the people of the valleys above this see the end and the beginning as one. Nay, they see neither "beginning" nor "end" and witness neither "first" nor "last". Nay rather, the denizens of the city of immortality, who dwell in the celestial garden, see not even "neither first nor last": They fly from all that is first and repulse all that is last. For these have passed over the worlds of names and, swift as lightning, fled beyond the worlds of attributes. Thus is it said: "The perfection of belief in Divine Unity is to deny Him any attributes."[31] And they [30]

25

have made their dwelling-place in the shadow of the Divine Essence.

31   Wherefore <u>Kh</u>ájih 'Abdu'lláh[32]—may God the Most High sanctify his blessed soul—hath made, in this connection, a subtle point and spoken an eloquent word as to the meaning of "Guide Thou us on the straight path",[33] which is: "Show us the right way; that is, honour us with the love of Thine Essence, that we may be freed from occupation with ourselves and aught else save Thee, and may become wholly Thine; that we may know only Thee, and see only Thee, and think of none save Thee."

32   Nay, they would even soar above this station, as it is said: "Love is a veil betwixt the lover and beloved." "More than this I am not permitted to tell."

33   At this hour the morn of true knowledge hath dawned and the lamps of wayfaring and wandering have been quenched.

> Veiled from this was Moses too,
> Despite His virtue and His light.
> Then thou who hast no wings at all,
> Abandon any hope of flight![34]

If thou be a man of communion and prayer, 34 soar upon the wings of assistance from the holy ones, that thou mayest behold the mysteries of the Friend and attain the lights of the Beloved: "Verily, we are God's, and to Him shall we return."[35]

After passing through the Valley of Knowl- 35 edge, which is the last station of limitation, the wayfarer cometh to THE FIRST STATION OF UNITY and drinketh from the cup of oneness, and gazeth upon the manifestations of singleness. In this station he pierceth the veils of plurality, fleeth the realms of the flesh, and ascendeth unto the heaven of unity. With the ear of God he heareth; with the eye of God he beholdeth the mysteries of divine creation. He steppeth into the inner sanctuary of the Friend and, as an intimate, shareth the pavilion of the Well-Beloved. He stretcheth forth the hand of truth from the sleeve of the Absolute and revealeth the mysteries of divine power. He seeth in himself neither name nor fame nor rank, but findeth his own praise in the praise of God, and in the name of God beholdeth his own. To him "all songs are from that sovereign King" and every melody from Him. He sitteth on the throne of "Say, all things are of God"[36] and reclineth upon the seat of "There is no power nor strength

THE CALL OF THE DIVINE BELOVED

but in God alone."[37] He looketh upon all things with the eye of Unity, and seeth the effulgent rays of the Sun of Truth shining from the dayspring of the Divine Essence upon all created things alike, and beholdeth the lights of Unity reflected upon all creation.

36 It is known to thine eminence that all the variations which the wayfarer in the stages of his journey beholdeth in the realms of being proceed from his own vision. We shall give an example of this, that the meaning may become fully clear. Consider the visible sun: Although it shineth with the same radiance upon all existence, and at the behest of the Lord of Revelation bestoweth light on all things, yet in each place it becometh manifest and sheddeth its bounty according to the potentialities of that place. For instance, in a mirror it reflecteth its own disk and shape, and this is due to the clarity of the mirror itself; through a crystal it maketh fire to appear; and in other things it showeth only the effect of its shining, but not its full disk. And yet, through that effect, by the command of the Creator it traineth each thing according to the capacity of that thing, even as thou dost observe.

37 In like manner, colours become visible in each

28

object according to its nature. For instance, in a yellow glass the rays shine yellow; in a white glass they are white; and in a red glass red rays are visible. These variations proceed from the object itself, not from the light. And if a place be shut away from the light, as by walls and a roof, it will be entirely bereft of the light of the sun and deprived of its rays.

Thus it is that certain feeble souls have confined [38] the wide expanse of knowledge within the walls of self and passion, and beneath the cloak of ignorance and blindness, and have thereby veiled themselves from the light of the mystic Sun and the mysteries of the eternal Beloved. They have strayed far from the gem-like wisdom of the resplendent Faith of the Lord of the Messengers,[38] have been shut out of the inner court of the All-Beauteous, and have been banished from the Kaaba of glory. Such is the worth of the people of this age!

And if a nightingale soar beyond the clay of [39] self and dwell in the rose bower of the heart, and in Arabian melodies and sweet Persian tones recount the mysteries of God—a single word whereof quickeneth anew every lifeless form and bestoweth the spirit of holiness upon every mouldering bone—thou wilt behold a thousand claws of envy and a myriad talons of hatred hunting after Him and striving with all their power to encompass His death.

40 Yea, to the beetle a sweet fragrance seemeth foul, and to the man sick of a rheum a pleasant perfume availeth naught. Wherefore hath it been said for the guidance of the ignorant:

> Cleanse thou the rheum from out thine
>   head
> And breathe the breath of God instead.[39]

41 In sum, the differences among objects have now been made plain. Thus when the wayfarer gazeth only upon the place of appearance— that is, when he considereth only the glass—he seeth yellow and red and white. And so it is that conflict hath prevailed amongst men, and a darksome dust from limited souls hath settled over the world. Others gaze upon the effulgence of the light, while yet others have drunk of the wine of oneness and see naught but the sun itself.

42 As the wayfarers traverse these three differing planes, their understanding and their words differ accordingly, and hence the sign of conflict hath

ever appeared on earth. For there are some who dwell on the plane of Divine Unity and speak of that world, and some inhabit the realms of limitation, and some the grades of self, while others are completely veiled. Thus do the ignorant people of the day, who have no share of the radiance of the divine Beauty, make certain claims and, in every age and cycle, inflict upon the people of the ocean of Divine Unity what they themselves deserve. "If God should chastise men for their perverse doings, He would not leave upon the earth a moving thing! But to an appointed time doth He respite them."[40]

O My brother! A pure heart is as a mirror; [43] cleanse it with the burnish of love and severance from all save God, that the true sun may shine therein and the eternal morning dawn. Then wilt thou clearly see the meaning of "Earth and heaven cannot contain Me; what can alone contain Me is the heart of him that believeth in Me."[41] And thou wilt take up thy life in thy hand and with infinite longing cast it before thy newly found Beloved.

Whensoever the light of the revelation of the [44] King of Oneness settleth upon the throne of the heart and soul, His radiance becometh visible in every limb and member. At that time, the mystery of the famed tradition gleameth out of the darkness: "A servant is drawn unto Me in prayer until I answer him, and when I have answered him, I become the ear wherewith he heareth …"[42] For thus the Master of the house hath appeared within His home, and all the pillars of the dwelling are ashine with His light. And as the action and effect of the light are from the Light-Giver, so it is that all move through Him and arise by His will. This is that wellspring whereof the near ones drink, as it is said: "A fount whereof they who draw nigh to God shall drink".[43]

45   However, let none construe these utterances to imply the incarnation or descent of the worlds of God into the grades of His creatures, nor should they lead thine eminence to such misapprehensions. For God, in His Essence, is sanctified above all ascent and descent, egress and regress; He hath through all eternity been exalted beyond the attributes of His creation, and will ever remain so. No man hath ever known Him; no soul hath ever fathomed the nature of His Being. In the valley of His knowledge every mystic wandereth astray; in the comprehension of His Essence every saint standeth bewildered. Sanctified is He above the understanding of the wise; exalted is

He beyond the knowledge of the knowing! "The
way is barred and all seeking rejected. His proof is
His signs, His evidence His being."[44]

Wherefore the lovers of the countenance of   46
the Beloved have said, "O Thou Whose Essence
alone can lead to His Essence, and Who transcen-
deth all likeness to His creatures".[45] How can utter
nothingness spur its charger in the arena of eternity, or a fleeting shadow reach to the everlasting
sun? The Friend addressed by the words "But for
Thee" hath said, "We have failed to know Thee";
and the Beloved alluded to by the words "or even
closer" hath said, "nor attained Thy presence".[46]

Indeed, the references that have been made to   47
the degrees of mystic knowledge pertain to the
knowledge of the effulgences of that Sun of Truth
as it becometh reflected in various mirrors. And
the effulgence of that light is present within the
hearts, yet it is hidden beneath the veils of selfish
desires and earthly attachments, even as a candle
within a lantern of iron, and only when the cover
is lifted doth the light of the candle shine out.

In like manner, when thou dost strip the veils   48
of illusion from the face of thine heart, the lights
of Oneness will be made manifest.

It is clear, then, that even these rays are not   49

subject to egress or regress—how much less that Essence of existence and longed-for Mystery. O My brother, consider these matters in the spirit of enquiry, not in blind imitation. A true wayfarer will not be deterred by the impediment of words, nor daunted by the sway of insinuations.

> How can a curtain part the lover from
>   his love,
> When Alexander's wall cannot keep
>   them apart?[47]

50   Secrets are many, and strangers are myriad. Volumes will not suffice to hold the mystery of the Beloved, nor can it be exhausted in these pages, though it be no more than a word, no more than a sign. "Knowledge is one point, which the foolish have multiplied."[48]

51   Infer, then, from this the differences among the worlds. Though the worlds of God be infinite, yet some refer to them as four: the world of time, which hath both a beginning and an end; the world of duration, which hath a beginning but whose end is not apparent; the world of primordial reality, whose beginning is not to be seen but which is known to have an end; and the world of

eternity, of which neither the beginning nor the end is visible. Although there are many differing statements as to these points, to recount them in detail would result in weariness. Thus some have said that the world of perpetuity hath neither beginning nor end, and have equated the world of eternity with the invisible, inaccessible, and unknowable Essence. Others have called these the worlds of the Heavenly Court, of the Celestial Dominion, of the Divine Kingdom, and of Mortal Existence.

Moreover, the journeys in the pathway of love have been reckoned as four: from the creatures to the True One, from the True One to the creatures, from the creatures to the creatures, and from the True One to the True One. 52

There is many an utterance of the sages and mystics of former times which I have not mentioned here, since I mislike copious citation from the sayings of the past; for quotation from the words of others betokeneth acquired learning and not divine bestowal. Even so much as I have quoted here is out of deference to the wont of men and after the manner of the learned. Further, such matters are beyond the scope of this epistle. My unwillingness to recount 53 their sayings is not from pride; rather, it is the manifestation of wisdom and the revelation of bounty.

> If <u>Kh</u>iḍr did wreck the vessel on the sea,
> A thousand rights are in this wrong
> concealed.[49]

54   Otherwise, this Servant regardeth Himself as utterly lost and non-existent, even before one of the beloved of God, how much less in the presence of His holy ones. Glorified be my Lord, the Most High! Moreover, our aim is to recount the stages of the wayfarer's journey, not to set forth the conflicting utterances of the mystics.

55   Although a brief example hath been given concerning the beginning and ending of the relative and contingent world, yet a further illustration is now provided, that the full meaning may become clear. For instance, let thine eminence consider his own self: Thou art first in relation to thy son, and last in relation to thy father. In thine outward appearance thou tellest of the appearance of power in the realms of divine creation; in thine inward being thou revealest the hidden mysteries

which are the divine trust deposited within thee.
And thus firstness and lastness, outwardness and
inwardness, are, in the sense referred to, all true of
thyself, so that in these four states conferred upon
thee thou mayest comprehend the four divine
states, and that the nightingale of thine heart,
warbling on all the flowering branches of the tree
of existence, whether seen or unseen, might cry
out: "He is the First and the Last, the Seen and
the Hidden!"[50]

These statements are made in the sphere of   56
that which is relative. Otherwise, those souls who
with but one step have traversed the world of
the relative and the conditioned, and dwelt in the
court of independent sovereignty, and pitched
their tent in the realms of absolute authority and
command, have burned away these relativities
with a single spark, and blotted out these words
with a mere dewdrop. And they swim in the sea
of the spirit, and soar in the holy atmosphere of
light. Then what existence have words, on such
a plane, that "first" and "last", or other than these,
should be mentioned or described? In this realm,
the first is the same as the last, and the last is the
same as the first.

In thy soul, of love build thou a fire
And burn all thoughts and words entire.[51]

57 O My friend, look to thyself: Hadst thou not become a father and begotten a son, neither wouldst thou have comprehended these words. Now forget them one and all, that thou mayest learn from the Master of Love in the school-house of Divine Unity, mayest return unto God, forsake the land of unreality for thy true station, and dwell beneath the shadow of the tree of knowledge.

58 O thou dear one! Impoverish thyself, that thou mayest enter the lofty court of riches; and humble thy body, that thou mayest drink from the stream of glory and attain to the full meaning of the poems whereof thou hadst asked.

59 Thus it hath been made clear that these stages depend on the attainment of the wayfarer. In every city he will behold a world, in every valley reach a spring, in every meadow hear a song. But the falcon of the mystic heaven hath many a wondrous carol of the spirit in its breast, and the Persian bird keepeth in its soul many a sweet Arabian melody; yet these are hidden, and hidden shall remain.

If I speak forth, many a mind will shatter,
And if I write, many a pen will break.[52]

Peace be upon him who concludeth this 60
exalted journey and followeth the way of truth
by the lights of guidance.

The wayfarer, after traversing the high planes 61
of this supernal journey, entereth into THE CITY
OF CONTENTMENT. In this valley he feeleth the
breezes of divine contentment blowing from the
plane of the spirit. He burneth away the veils of
want, and with inward and outward eye perceiveth
within and without all things the day of "God
will satisfy everyone out of His abundance."[53]
From sorrow he turneth to bliss, and from grief
to joy, and from anguish and dejection to delight
and rapture.

Although, to outward seeming, the wayfarers in 62
this valley may dwell upon the dust, yet inwardly
they are throned in the heights of mystic meaning;
they partake of the eternal bounties of heaven and
drink of the delicate wines of the spirit.

The tongue faileth in describing these three 63
valleys, and speech falleth short. The pen steppeth
not into this arena, the ink leaveth only a blot. In
these stations, the nightingale of the heart hath

other songs and secrets, which make the heart to leap and the soul to cry out, but this mystery of inner meaning may be whispered only from heart to heart, and confided only from breast to breast.

> The bliss of mystic knowers can be only
> told from heart to heart,
> A bliss no messenger can bear and no
> missive dare impart.[54]

> How many are the matters I have out of
> weakness left unsaid;
> For my words would fail to reckon them
> and mine every effort would fall short.[55]

[64] O friend, till thou enter the garden of these inner meanings, thou shalt never taste of the imperishable wine of this valley. And shouldst thou taste of it, thou wilt turn away from all else and drink of the cup of contentment; thou wilt loose thyself from all things and bind thyself unto Him, and lay down thy life in His path and offer up thy soul for His sake. And this, even though in this realm there is no "all else" that thou needst forget: "God was alone; there was none else besides Him."[56] For on this plane the traveller

witnesseth the beauty of the Friend in all things.
In fire he seeth the face of the Beloved; in illusion
he beholdeth the secret of reality; in the attributes
he readeth the riddle of the Essence. For he hath
burnt away all veils with a sigh, and cast aside all
coverings with a glance. With piercing sight he
gazeth upon the new creation, and with lucid
heart he graspeth subtle verities. The words "And
we have made thy sight sharp in this day"[57] are
a sufficient proof of this assertion and a befitting
description of this state.

After journeying through the planes of pure 65
contentment, the traveller cometh to THE VALLEY
OF WONDERMENT and is tossed upon the oceans
of grandeur, and at every moment his wonder
increaseth. Now he seeth the embodiment of
wealth as poverty itself, and the essence of inde-
pendence as sheer impotence. Now is he struck
dumb with the beauty of the All-Glorious; again
is he wearied out with his own life. How many a
mystic tree hath this whirlwind of bewilderment
snatched by the roots, how many a soul hath it
worn out and exhausted. For in this valley the
traveller is flung into confusion, albeit, in the eyes
of him who hath attained, such signs are esteemed
and well beloved. At every moment, he beholdeth

41

a wondrous world and a new creation, and goeth from astonishment to astonishment, and is lost in awe before the new handiwork of Him Who is the sovereign Lord of all.

66   Indeed, O brother, if we ponder each created thing, we shall witness a myriad consummate wisdoms and learn a myriad new and wondrous truths. One of the created phenomena is the dream. Behold how many secrets have been deposited therein, how many wisdoms treasured up, how many worlds concealed. Observe how thou art asleep in a dwelling, and its doors are shut; on a sudden thou findest thyself in a far-off city, which thou enterest without moving thy feet or wearying thy body. Without taxing thine eyes, thou seest; without troubling thine ears, thou hearest; without a tongue, thou speakest. And perchance when ten years have passed, thou wilt witness in this temporal world the very things thou hast dreamt tonight.

67   Now there are many wisdoms to ponder in the dream, which none but the people of this valley can comprehend in their reality. First, what is this world where without eye or ear or hand or tongue one can put all these to use? Second, how is it that in the outer world thou seest today the

effect of a dream which thou didst witness in
the world of sleep some ten years past? Consider
the difference between these two worlds, and the
mysteries they conceal, that, attended by divine
confirmations, thou mayest attain unto heavenly
discoveries and enter the realms of holiness.

God, the Most High, hath placed these signs 68
in men so that veiled minds might not deny the
mysteries of the life beyond, nor belittle that
which hath been promised them. For some hold
fast to reason and deny whatever reason comprehendeth not, and yet feeble minds can never
grasp the reality of the stages that we have related:
The universal divine Intellect alone can comprehend them.

How can feeble reason embrace the Qur'án
Or the spider snare a phoenix in its web?[58]

All these states are to be found and witnessed 69
in the Valley of Wonderment, wherein the wayfarer at every moment seeketh for more and is not
wearied. Thus the Lord of the first and the last,[59]
in setting forth the grades of contemplation and
expressing bewilderment, hath said: "Increase my
wonder and amazement at Thee, O God!"[60]

43

70 Likewise, reflect upon the perfection of man's creation, and that all these planes and states are folded up and hidden away within him.

> Dost thou deem thyself a small and
>   puny form,
> When thou foldest within thyself the
>   greater world?

71 We must therefore labour to destroy the animal condition, till the meaning of humanity cometh to light.

72 Likewise, Luqmán, who had drunk from the wellspring of wisdom and tasted of the waters of mercy, in proving to his son Nathan the planes of resurrection and death, advanced the dream as evidence and example. We relate it here, that through this evanescent Servant a memory may endure of that youth of the school of Divine Unity, that elder of the realms of instruction and detachment. He said: "O son, if thou art able not to sleep, then thou art able not to die. And if thou art able not to waken after sleep, then thou shalt be able not to rise after death."

73 O friend, the heart is the dwelling-place of eternal mysteries: Make it not the home of fleeting

fancies. Waste not the treasure of thy precious life occupied with this swiftly passing world. Thou comest from the world of holiness: Bind not thine heart to the earth. Thou art a dweller in the court of reunion: Choose not the homeland of the dust.

In sum, there is no end to the description of these stages, but because of the wrongs inflicted by the peoples of this age, this Servant is disinclined to continue: 74

> The tale remaineth yet unfinished
>   and untold;
> Forgive me, then, for weariness hath
>   taken hold.[61]

The pen groaneth and the ink sheddeth tears, and the river of the heart surgeth in waves of blood. "Nothing can befall us but what God hath destined for us."[62] Peace be upon him who followeth the way of guidance! 75

After scaling the high summits of wonderment, the wayfarer cometh to THE VALLEY OF TRUE POVERTY AND ABSOLUTE NOTHINGNESS. This station is that of dying to the self and living in God, of being poor in self and rich in the Desired One. Poverty, as here referred to, signifieth being 76 poor in that which pertaineth to the world of creation and rich in what belongeth to the realms of God. For when the true lover and devoted friend reacheth the presence of the Beloved, the radiant beauty of the Loved One and the fire of the lover's heart will kindle a blaze and burn away all veils and wrappings. Yea, all that he hath, from marrow to skin, will be set aflame, so that nothing will remain save the Friend.

> When once shone forth the attributes
> Of Him Who is the ancient King,
> All mention Moses burned away
> Of every fleeting, transient thing.[63]

77   Whoso hath attained this station is sanctified from all that pertaineth to the world. Wherefore, if those who have reached the ocean of His presence are found to possess none of the limited things of this perishable world, whether earthly riches or worldly opinions, it mattereth not. For that which is with His creatures is circumscribed by their own limitations, whereas that which is with God is sanctified therefrom. This utterance must be deeply pondered, that its purport may be clear. "Verily the righteous shall drink of a cup

46

tempered at the camphor fountain."[64] If the true meaning of "camphor" become known, our true intent will become evident.

This station is that poverty of which it is said, "Poverty is My glory."[65] And of inward and outward poverty there is many a stage and many a meaning which I have not thought pertinent to mention here; hence I have reserved these for another time, dependent on what God may desire and fate may seal.

This is the station wherein the multiplicity of all things perisheth in the wayfarer; and the divine Countenance, dawning above the horizon of eternity, riseth out of the darkness; and the meaning of "All on the earth shall pass away, but the face of thy Lord" is made manifest.[66]

O My friend! Listen with heart and soul to the songs of the spirit, and treasure them as thine own eyes; for heavenly wisdoms, even as vernal showers, will not rain forever upon the earth of men's hearts, and though the grace of the All-Bounteous One is never ceasing and never stilled, yet to every time and era a portion is allotted and a bounty assigned, which is vouchsafed in a given measure. "And no one thing is there, but with Us are its storehouses; and We send it not down but in settled measure."[67] Indeed, the clouds of the Loved One's mercy rain only on the garden of the spirit, and bestow this bounty only in the season of spring. Other seasons have no share in this supernal grace, and barren lands hold no portion of this bounteous favour.

81   O My brother! Not every sea hath pearls; not every branch will flower, nor will the nightingale sing thereon. Then, ere the nightingale of the mystic Paradise repair to the celestial garden, and the rays of the morn of inner meaning return to the Day-Star of Truth, make thou an effort, that haply in this dust-heap of a mortal world thou mayest catch a fragrance from the everlasting rose-garden and live in the shadow of the inhabitants of this everlasting city. And when thou hast attained this highest plane and most exalted degree, then shalt thou gaze on the Beloved and forget all else.

> The Friend, unveiled, doth shed the splendour
>   of His light
> Through every door and wall, O ye endued
>   with sight![68]

82   Thou hast given up the drop of life and drawn nigh unto the ocean of the Well-Beloved. This is

the goal thou didst seek; God grant thou mayest attain thereunto.

In this city, even the veils of light are rent asunder and vanish away. "His beauty hath no veiling save light, His countenance no covering save revelation."[69] How strange that the Beloved is as visible as the sun and yet the heedless still hunt after tinsel and base metal. Yea, the intensity of His revelation hath veiled Him, and the fullness of His shining forth hath hidden Him. 83

Even as the noontide sun
Hath the True One brightly shined,
But alas that He hath come
To the city of the blind![70]

In this valley the wayfarer passeth beyond the stages of the "unity of existence" and the "unity of appearance" and reacheth a unity that is sanctified above both of these stations.[71] Ecstasy alone can encompass this theme, not utterance nor argument; and whosoever hath dwelt at this stage of the journey, or caught a breath from this garden, knoweth whereof We speak. 84

In all these journeys the wayfarer must stray not a hair's breadth from the Law, for this is indeed 85

49

the secret of the Path and the fruit of the Tree of Truth. And in all these stages he must cling to the robe of obedience to all that hath been enjoined, and hold fast to the cord of shunning all that is forbidden, that he may partake of the cup of the Law and be informed of the mysteries of Truth.

86   If any of the utterances of this Servant be not understood, or lead to perplexity, the same must be enquired of again, that no doubt may linger, and that the meaning may shine as resplendent as the face of the Beloved dawning from His "Glorious Station".[72]

87   These journeys have no visible ending in this temporal world, but the detached wayfarer—should invisible confirmation descend upon him and the Guardian of the Cause assist him—may traverse these seven stages in seven steps, nay rather in seven breaths, nay even in a single breath, should God will and desire it.[73] This is "a token of His grace vouchsafed unto whomsoever He pleaseth."[74]

88   They who soar in the heaven of Divine Unity and attain the depths of the sea of detachment reckon this city—which is the station of life in God—as the loftiest state of the mystic knowers and the furthermost homeland of the faithful

lovers. But to this evanescent One of the mystic ocean, this station is the first gate of the heart's citadel, that is, man's first entrance to the city of the heart; and the heart is endowed with four stages, which would be recounted should a kindred soul be found.

> Shattered was the pen at once,
> Rent and torn in twain the page,
> When the pen did reach the point
> Of depicting such a stage.[75]

∞

O My friend! Many a hound hunteth this [89] gazelle of the desert of oneness; many an eagle pursueth this nightingale of the garden of eternity. Ravens of hatred lie in wait for this bird of the heavens of God, and the huntsman of envy stalketh this deer of the meadow of love.

O Shaykh! Make of thine effort a glass, that [90] perchance it may shelter this flame from contrary winds, albeit this flame doth long to be kindled in the lamp of the Lord and to shine in the niche of the spirit. For the head that is raised up in the love of God will assuredly fall by the sword, and the life that is aflame with longing will assuredly be extinguished, and the heart that cleaveth to the remembrance of the Beloved will assuredly break. How well hath it been said:

> Live free of love, for its peace
> Is grief and sorrow at each breath.
> It starteth but with ache and pain;
> It endeth but with loss and death.[76]

Peace be upon him who followeth the way of guidance!

91   The novel thoughts thou hast expressed as to the symbolism contained in the word "sparrow" were considered.[77] Thou appearest to be well grounded in mystic truth. However, in each realm, to every letter a meaning is allotted which pertaineth to that realm. Indeed, the wayfarer findeth a secret in every name and a mystery in every letter.

92   In one sense, these letters refer to the states of holiness. The first meaneth "Free thyself from the promptings of self, then approach thy Lord." The second meaneth "Purify thyself from all save Him, that thou mayest offer up thy life for His sake." The third meaneth "Draw back from

the threshold of the one true God if thou art still possessed of earthly attributes." The fourth meaneth "Render thanks unto thy Lord on His earth, that He may bless thee in His heaven, albeit in the realm of His unity His heaven is the same as His earth." The fifth meaneth "Remove from thine eyes the veils of limitation, that thou mayest learn that which thou knewest not of the stations of holiness."

Wert thou to hearken unto the melodies of 93 this mortal Bird, then wouldst thou seek out the eternal and undying chalice and renounce every fleeting and perishable cup. Peace be upon him who followeth the way of guidance!

3

From the Letter Bá'
to the Letter Há'

IN THE NAME OF OUR LORD, THE MOST
EXALTED, THE MOST HIGH!

I ADDRESSED UNTO THEE aforetime an Epistle   1
in the lucid Arabian tongue, and I now reveal
for thee this Tablet in wondrous Persian prose,
that thou mayest hear, in the glorious accents of
the Nightingale of 'Iráq, the sweet melodies of
the nearness of the heavenly Paradise that had,
ere this, been intoned in the language of Ḥijáz.[78]
Perchance thou mayest become pure spirit;
attain, without taking a single step, the loftiest
stations of mystic ascent; and explore, without
leaving thine outward habitation, the furthermost reaches of the worlds of inner significance.
Thereupon wouldst thou, with a divine rapture,
experience true spiritual attraction, lay down thy
life in the path of the Friend, and sacrifice thy
soul in the wilderness of His love. This indeed
is the meaning of stillness in flight and flight

57

in stillness, of fluidity in solidity and solidity in fluidity.

2   To continue: It is clear that the wayfarers in the wilderness of search and longing, of attainment and reunion, have numerous degrees and count-less stations. Some, after spiritual struggle and physical toil, ascend from the lower reaches of "no God is there" to the lofty bowers of "but God",[79] flee from the shadow of negation to abide in the limitless realm of affirmation, and abandon the privation of a transient existence for the bountiful assemblage of reunion. This is the uttermost limit of the realm of effort and striving.

3   Others, without receiving the least intimation of "no God is there", pass beyond the highest horizon of "but God"; without even tasting a dewdrop of the degrees of self-surrender ascend unto the kingdom of life everlasting; and without partaking from the wellspring of utter abnegation quaff the wine of the Ancient of Days. These souls, as they traverse the stages of wayfaring and ascend unto the stations of reunion, walk a different path and occupy a different rank.

4   Still others, without having perused a single letter of the kingdom of names or acquired the faintest intimation from the realm of attributes,

which pertaineth to this world, dawn above the
invisible horizon of eternity and return again
thereunto. A hundred thousand seas of glory
surge in their luminous hearts, and yet to outward
seeming their lips are parched; a myriad rivers of
holiness stream within their breasts, and yet no
trace thereof is to be seen; the books of God's
consummate wisdom are recorded upon the
tablets of their hearts, and yet they breathe not a
word thereof in the world of appearances. They
dwell in the Egypt of certitude and journey in the
lands of resignation. They are intoxicated with the
beauty, and entranced by the glory, of Him Who
is the All-Glorious. Heart to heart they whisper
hidden secrets; soul to soul they unfold abstruse
matters. The mysteries of the Divine Essence
glow upon their brows, and the lights of Divine
Unity shine from their peerless faces. They clothe
themselves in the robe of concealment and cast
their sleeves over both this world and the world
to come. Without wings they soar, without feet
they walk, without hands they grasp and hold.
They speak an unknown tongue and observe an
unseen grammar, of which all the world's inhabitants know not a single letter, save those whom
thy Lord hath willed. Unto each hath a share been

vouchsafed in His Book, and they shall all attain unto that which hath been destined for them.

5   It is clear and evident that, in this Dispensation wherein the banner of utterance hath been raised aloft and the candle of discernment hath been lit, there is no Lord but the Exalted One.[80] He it is Who is one in His essence and one in His attributes, single in the kingdom of names and peerless in the realm of actions. It is by virtue of His blessed name that the seas of Divine Unity have been made to surge; it is through the power of His resistless command that the immutable decrees of destiny have been enforced; it is through the potency of His sovereign might that the dictates of fate have been fixed. Who hath the power to soar in that exalted atmosphere or to cherish another beloved than Him? We all abide beneath His shadow and seek our portion from the ocean of His grace. However far the gnat may fly, it can never traverse the length and breadth of heaven, and however high the sparrow may soar, it can never attain the tree of immortality.

6   But since all do not possess the same degree of spiritual understanding, certain statements will inevitably be made, and there shall arise, as a consequence, as many differing opinions as there

are human minds, and as many divergent beliefs as there are created things. This is certain and settled, and can in no wise be averted. Now, it is clear that some are virtuous, others are sinful, and still others are rebellious. One must call the people to love and faithfulness, to zeal and contentment, that the sinful may be admonished and the ranks of the virtuous may swell. Nor is it possible that there be no sinners: So long as the name "the Ever-Forgiving" shineth resplendent above the horizon of existence, there will be sinners in the world of creation, for the latter cannot appear without the former and the former cannot exist without the latter.

Our aim is that thou shouldst urge all the believers to show forth kindness and mercy and to overlook certain shortcomings among them, that differences may be dispelled; true harmony be established; and the censure and reproach, the hatred and dissension, seen among the peoples of former times may not arise anew. Perchance they may be educated and, in the latter Resurrection,[81] inflict not upon that cherished Spirit and Essence of existence, that exalted and subtle Reality, the least of that which the Point of the Bayán was made to suffer.

61

8   Moreover, a reply to thine enquiries was sent aforetime. It is evident that whatever question is asked will be answered through the ocean of eternal grace, but such questions also add to the burden of duties imposed upon the servants. That which hath been recorded at God's behest in the Persian Bayán is indeed sufficient unto all, and none will be held to account for what it hath not commanded. Consider how numerous were those in the early days of the Revelation who obeyed, without the slightest deviation, every least one of its injunctions and yet reaped no benefit therefrom. The beginning of religion is love for God and for His Chosen Ones, and its end is to manifest that love to His servants.

9   I swear by God! Whoso faileth to obey the commandments of God can in no wise be numbered among His loved ones, for among the conditions of His love is to follow His commandments and observe His prohibitions. But since these are the days of concealment, and the Sun of eternity remaineth hidden beneath the horizon of being, one must gather together everyone with love and protect them. The time for the completion of the commandments and the perfection of deeds will assuredly come.

Three Other Tablets

4

O FRIEND! Many a day hath passed, and still 1 the sweet fragrance of thy faithfulness hath failed to reach Us. Hast thou forgotten the One Who forgetteth thee not, and forsaketh thee not, and neglecteth thee not, even as thou hast forgotten, forsaken, and neglected Him?

We have heard that sorrows have compassed 2 thee round in these days. Thy sorrow hath grieved Us, and that which hath befallen thee hath touched Us with bitter pain and anguish. But at this moment, O friend, the Herald of eternity announceth unto thee, by the robe of faithfulness, His joyful tidings and bestoweth upon thee this emerald-green Tablet. Set out, then, from thine abode, take thou seven steps upon the earth, and with each step complete a stage of the journey.

3   With the first, enter the ocean of search and seek God, thy Lord, with thine inmost heart and soul.

4   With the second, enter the ocean of love and make mention of God, thy Lord, in the transports of thy longing and the ecstasies of thy rapture.

5   With the third, tread the paths of detachment; that is, sever thyself from thine idle fancies and walk in the ways of thy Lord.

6   With the fourth, enter the fathomless depths of oneness and the billowing seas of eternity. Cover thy face in the dust before the Lord of Lords, and sanctify thy self and thy spirit from all departure and return, that thine inmost heart may be freed from all things in the kingdoms of creation.

7   With the fifth, ascend unto the heaven of wonderment, that thou mayest taste the goodly fruits of this blessed realm, lose thyself in bewilderment before the power of thy Beloved and the dominion of thy Creator, and proclaim that which the King of existence and the Goal of all desire hath proclaimed: "Increase my wonder and amazement at Thee, O God!"[82]

8   With the sixth, soar upon the wings of submission and contentment unto the cities of the Unseen, that thou mayest enter the expanses of

utter nothingness wherein thou shalt die to thy self and live in Him Who hath fashioned thee.

With the seventh, drown thyself in the depths 9 of eternity, that death may not overtake thee, and that thou mayest abide forever in the shadow of the everlasting Face of God. Thereupon shall the fragrance of the All-Glorious be diffused from the realm of the All-Merciful, and thy heart shall grieve no more over the vicissitudes of a fleeting life and the turns of a transient fortune.

When once thou hast privily completed these 10 journeys, place this robe upon thy sightless eyes, that the eye of thine inmost heart may be opened. By God, O My friend! Wert thou to attain unto this station, thou wouldst find wondrous worlds; discover heavenly bowers, celestial gardens, and transcendent realms; and unravel the secrets of the progress of the souls of men through the atmosphere of eternal holiness and the heavens of imperishable glory. Thou wouldst so rejoice within thy soul as to cause the signs of joy and gladness to appear throughout the whole earth. Thereafter, sorrow would never again hold sway over thee, nor would grief ever seize thee in its grasp, for thou wouldst abide in the heaven of holiness amidst the concourse of the blissful.

11   Know thou, moreover, that in the sight of God thou holdest a lofty rank and an exalted station. Remove not thyself from the company of His servants; rather do thou gather them together in the Cause of God and admonish them in His days. Rely upon God in all thine affairs. He, verily, shall suffice thee in all things, shall protect thee from the followers of the Evil One, and shall cause thee to enter the everlasting Paradise, wherein thou shalt be numbered with the blessed. Convey, then, Our greetings unto those who follow thee in the Cause of thy Lord, and summon them unto the Straight Path.

5

O SHAMS! Hearken with all thy heart unto the nightingale song of the Beloved, that perchance thou mayest abandon the habitation of self and desire and step into the placeless realm of eternal glory, forsake thine own life, and commune with Him Who is the life of thy life. Wert thou to traverse the limitless reaches of the spirit, thou wouldst of a certainty rend asunder the garment of patience and forbearance, hasten to offer up thy soul, renounce the dross of this fleeting world, and find repose upon the throne of ancient glory.

Each thing must needs have an effect and each sign reveal a secret. Not until the world-illuming sun hath shone can the east be distinguished from the west, nor the blooming garden discerned from the barren waste. Heavenly strains compare not with earthly clamours, and the croaking of the raven can in no wise be confounded with the song of the nightingale. For the latter bespeaketh the land of the Beloved and increaseth life, whereas the former telleth only of the city of the blind and causeth faith to wither.

3   One must step forth and raise aloft the banner of earnest striving. By God! Wert thou to hearken unto the heavenly words of this evanescent Servant that have been raised in this mystic Tablet, thou wouldst assuredly take to the desert of self-surrender, turn aside from thine own heart and soul, and cast thy head at the feet of the Friend. How high is the soaring flight of the phoenix of love, and how low the requisite measure of our yearning! Strive but a little to soar, that, by the grace of Him Who is the eternal King, thou mayest ascend from the dust-heap of utter non-existence unto the loftiest heights of ancient glory. Give wings to thy celestial spirit and lend strength to thy mystic soul, that haply it may take flight in the atmosphere of divine nearness and attain the ultimate and invisible goal.

4   This profitless world produceth naught save deadly poison, and its ephemeral dregs can never yield the everlasting cup. Were the Jesus of the

spirit to give ear to the call of holiness from the Falcon of the realm above, He would assuredly cry out from His inmost being and be seized with fervid longing even as the lover's soul. It is through that call that the Moses of eternity was dumbfounded; it is by its virtue that the Abraham of faithfulness shattered the idol of the mortal body. Shatter then, in turn, this idol, that thou mayest take up thine abode in the land of the Beloved; and forsake all desire, that thou mayest take flight unto the Egypt of imperishable glory. Sanctify the city of thine heart, that thou mayest behold the beauty of the Divine Essence and be quickened to a new life through the grace of the Holy Spirit.

No melody remaineth that was not intoned 5 upon this branch; no song remaineth that this Nightingale hath not warbled. A thousand Arabian ears are powerless to fathom this Persian lament— nay, none but an embodiment of divine virtues can grasp this subtle mystery. Well it is, then, with the one who attaineth this ocean and drinketh therefrom the draught of life!

6

O thou lion-hearted soul,   1
Even as a lion roar,
That thy roaring may perchance
To the seventh heaven soar!⁸³

P RAISE BE to Him Whose Essence is immea-   2
surably exalted above the strivings of human
hearts, however pure, to soar into the atmosphere of His nearness, and Whose Being is
immensely sanctified beyond the exertions of
human minds, however lofty, to ascend unto the
heaven of His presence. From time immemorial
He hath been exalted above the description of
aught save Himself, and He will forever continue
to be sanctified beyond the praise of all created
things. The hearts of them that have recognized
Him are sore perplexed before the tokens of His
everlasting handiwork, and the minds of them
that have attained His court are bewildered by
the wondrous evidences of the Revealers of His

oneness. He, verily, is the All-Possessing, the Almighty, the Most Glorious, the Help in Peril, the Self-Subsisting.

3   O friend! Thine epistle was received. It told of naught save the fire which hath been kindled in the tree of human reality, and bore no message but that which bestoweth a new life upon enlightened hearts. Well is it with him that hath been set ablaze by the fire of thy love, and who hath quaffed the water of life from the cup of thine affection. "The righteous shall drink of a cup tempered at the camphor fountain."[84]

4   To continue: Thy letter, which was a repository of the pearls of celestial knowledge, was brought before this Exile. God be praised, it rolled up the scrolls of separation and remoteness and spread out in their stead the realms of nearness and reunion. Methinks through the water of thy longing the fire of separation was changed into "coolness and safety".[85] In truth, a perfect meeting was attained through thy letter, and, through thy mention of the stations of Divine Unity and the signs of pure abstraction and oneness, it lifted from the world the veils of limitation. And this, notwithstanding that even the limitations of the world of existence are

praised and cherished by the wayfarer, for he seeth all things in the mirror of the verse "No defect canst thou see in the creation of the God of mercy", and at every moment he heareth with his inner ear the tongue of the Holy Spirit uttering the words "Seest thou a single flaw?"[86] In faithlessness he beholdeth the secret of fidelity, and in deadly poison he tasteth the sweetest honey. Even vengeance is embraced in this state; nay more, the true lover welcometh the betrayal of the beloved.

> Thy faithlessness I cherish more
> Than every gift that life can give.
> To suffer at thy vengeful hand—
> How much dearer than to live![87]

Thus do the wayfarers in the wilderness of solitude and search experience events and conditions which, though to outward seeming be a mortal poison, are inwardly a wholesome draught, and though in appearance a passing mirage, are in reality pure and refreshing waters. Were I to attempt a full description of this station, neither could I express it nor the hearer grasp it. And whoso observeth with the eye of innate knowledge will confess, openly as well as privily, the selfsame truth.

6   As to perceived differences, these can be attributed to the divers stations that have been attained by them that tread the path of search and mystic knowledge. Thus, at one time the wayfarer beholdeth the lover hastening in search of the beloved through the wilderness of desolation, and at another he seeth the beloved yearning for the lover across the wilds of longing and devotion, or wandering, aimless and bewildered, the wastes of love in his pursuit.

> "O for a drop to drink!" the thirsty soul
>   doth groan;
> "O for a thirsty soul!" the spring in turn
>   doth moan.[88]

7   From yet another vantage he perceiveth that the lover and the beloved are one and the same, and that the seeker is himself the very object of his search. "How can the lover from the loved one ever part?"[89] So it is that, at times, the lovers of the celestial Beauty sound the clarion of "Say: All things are of God", while, at others, they raise the call of "It is from thyself."[90]

Some have related the aforementioned stages 8
to the inner and outer journeys of the soul,
which is the station of "the knowledge of certitude", whilst others that have quaffed the wine of
reunion regard each and every stage as relating to
that knowledge, and consider the two stations of
"the eye of certitude" and "the truth of certitude"
as being exalted above and sanctified beyond
these realms and all that pertaineth unto them,
even as hath been clearly affirmed by that mystic
knower.[91] For in all these stages the mirror of
the wayfarer's heart may bear the reflection of
shadowy desires, wayward thoughts, and worldly
attachments. Wherefore hath it been said that, in
these stations, at one time the hosts of reason are
triumphant and, at another, the armies of love
prevail. At one time, the clouds of affliction and
sorrow conceal the heavens of gladness and joy; at
another, the eternal leviathan of love devoureth,
in one fleeting moment, all manifestations of
sadness, anguish, grief, and dejection, and the
morn of divine guidance dawneth forth with the
joyful tidings of "despair not of God's mercy",[92]
and the gentle breezes of His providence dispel
every vestige of torpor and estrangement. These
tidings, however, are not constant and immutable

in these stations, and the wayfarer remaineth confined between the right hand of faith and assurance and the left hand of denial and despair.

9   Some wayfarers remain forever veiled in these stages. Others are assisted by invisible aid from the Source of unfailing grace, whereat the hosts of the Realm on high raise the tabernacle of divine power, and the ascendency of "and verily Our host shall conquer"[93] is manifested, obliterating the signs and standards of every worldly attachment and limitation, even as alluded to by some who have attained this station. At such times, the ascendency of God's names and attributes will so surround a soul as to leave it no place either to stay or to flee. This station, however, hath its own obscurities and impediments, for they that journey towards the land of Divine Unity and detachment are still wrapt within the confines of names and attributes, and take delight in their gardens and bowers. Thus it is that, in describing these stations, some have made reference to the "unity of existence" and the "unity of appearance".[94] By this is meant that the seeker will close his eyes to all save his Beloved and open them to naught but His beauty. He will pass beyond the mortal world and approach the everlasting

realm. He will see no beauty but the Beloved's and hear no utterance but His praise; that is, he will avert his gaze from aught save His beauty and refuse to hearken to any melody but the sweet accents of His voice. Howbeit some are led astray even in this station; for no sooner do they inhale the fragrance of reunion, and hearken unto the voice of the doves of heavenly grace, than they imagine themselves to have attained perfection and wander lost in the wilderness of self-conceit, thus depriving themselves of the soft-flowing stream of divine providence and the ethereal cup of heavenly delight.

Yet others, assisted by the grace of the ever-lasting Friend, consume these veils with the fire of His love and step into the meads of ancient glory. That is, forsaking the wilderness of the "unity of existence", they attain unto the ultimate abode of the "true appearance of the Divine Unity". So clearly will they witness in this stage God's all-encompassing mercy that in every created thing, both in the world and in the souls of men, they will behold Him Who hath been interpreted as the Holy Outpouring. No longer will they close their eyes to any beauty, nor stop their ears from hearkening to any voice. For there is no prohibition

79

in this stage and no debarment, inasmuch as in all things they will discern, with both their outer and inner eyes, the revelation of the signs of Him Who is the King of all names and attributes, and in every atom they will find a door that leadeth to the garden of Divine Unity and the city of pure abstraction. "Where'er I turn my gaze, 'tis Thee Whom I behold." So entirely will the hearts of the wayfarers be transported by longing for the ecstasies of this station that they will come to conceive no stage apart from this stage, to see themselves as abiding within the court of the Beloved and circling round His sanctuary, and to consider it as the ultimate abode of them that search and the uttermost station of such as have attained.

11   A myriad names and attributes have been ascribed to these degrees and stations, which I am disinclined to mention here. It is, indeed, solely because of thy longing and devotion that I have engaged in such ephemeral and limited topics. And this, notwithstanding that speech is the greatest evidence of the worth of the speaker and guideth unto the recognition of the source of guidance, for no more complete and enduring proof hath been or will be vouchsafed unto man from the empyrean of everlasting glory than words

and utterance. This, verily, is a self-evident truth, for the braying of the donkey can never compare with the cooing of the dove. Never wilt thou hear from the raven the melodies of the nightingale, nor inhale from the abject beetle the fragrance of eternity.

7

The Four Valleys

HE IS THE EVER-LIVING.

O light of truth and sword of faith   1
And soul of generosity!
No prince hath sky or earth begot
Who fain could hope to rival thee![95]

I KNOW NOT why the tie of love was so abruptly   2
severed and the firm covenant of friendship
broken. Did ever, God forbid, My devotion lessen
or My sincere affection fail, that I came to be so
neglected and forgotten?

What fault didst thou observe in me
That made thee cease thy tender care?
Is it that poverty's our lot
And wealth and pageantry thy share?[96]

Or is it that a single arrow hath driven thee from   3
the battle? Hast thou not heard that steadfastness

is the prime requisite of the mystic path and the means of admittance to His holy Court? "They that say 'Our Lord is God', and continue steadfast in His way, upon them, verily, shall the angels descend."[97]

4   Likewise He saith, "Be thou steadfast as thou hast been bidden."[98] It followeth that they that abide in the court of reunion must needs conduct themselves accordingly.

> I do as bidden and convey the message,
> Whether it give thee counsel or offence.[99]

5   Though I have received no reply to My letter, and it would be unbefitting, in the eyes of the wise, to express anew My devotion, yet this new love hath annulled and effaced all the old rules and ways.

> Tell us not the tale of Laylí, nor speak of
>   Majnún's woe—
> Thy love hath made the world forget the
>   loves of long ago.
> When once thy name was on the tongue, it
>   reached the lovers' ears

And set the speakers and the hearers
    dancing to and fro.[100]

And as to divine wisdom and heavenly 6
admonitions:

Each moon, O my belov'd,
For three days I go mad;
Today's the first of these—
'Tis why thou seest me glad.[101]

I hear that that thou hast journeyed to Tabríz 7
and Tiflis to engage in debate and instruction, or
hast set out for Sanandaj to scale the heights of
knowledge.

    O my eminent friend! They that seek to ascend 8
to the heaven of mystic wayfaring are of four
kinds only. I shall describe them in brief, that the
signs and degrees of each may become plain and
manifest to thee.

    If the wayfarers be among them that seek 9
after THE SANCTUARY OF THE DESIRED ONE, this
plane pertaineth to the self—but the self which
is intended is "the Self of God that pervadeth
all His laws".[102] In this station the self is not

rejected but beloved; it is regarded with favour and is not to be shunned. Although at the beginning this plane is the realm of conflict, yet it endeth in the ascent to the throne of glory. As it hath been said:

> O Abraham of the Spirit and God's Friend
> in this day!
> Slay! Slay these four thieving birds of prey![103]

that after death the mystery of life may be unravelled.

10   This is the plane of the soul that is pleasing unto God, whereof He saith: "Enter thou among My servants, and enter thou My Paradise."[104]

11   This station hath myriad signs and countless tokens. Hence it is said: "We will surely show them Our signs in the world and within themselves, until it become plain to them that there is no God save Him."[105]

12   One must, then, read the book of one's own self, rather than the treatise of some grammarian. Wherefore He hath said, "Read thy Book: There needeth none but thyself to make out an account against thee this day."[106]

13   The story is told of a mystic knower who

went on a journey with a learned grammarian for a companion. They came to the shore of the Sea of Grandeur. The knower, putting his trust in God, straightway flung himself into the waves, but the grammarian stood bewildered and lost in thoughts that were as words traced upon the water. The mystic called out to him, "Why dost thou not follow?" The grammarian answered, "O brother, what can I do? As I dare not advance, I must needs go back again." Then the mystic cried, "Cast aside what thou hast learned from Síbavayh and Qawlavayh, from Ibn-i-Ḥájib and Ibn-i-Málik, and cross the water!"[107]

> With renunciation, not with grammar's
>   rules, one must be armed:
> Be nothing, then, and cross this sea
>   unharmed.[108]

Likewise He saith, "And be ye not like those who forget God, and whom He hath therefore caused to forget their own selves. Such men are the evil doers."[109] 14

If the wayfarers be among them that dwell in THE COURT OF THE ALL-PRAISED, this is the station of the Intellect, which is known as the messenger 15 of the realm of the body and the most great pillar. That which is intended, however, is the universal divine Intellect, whose sovereignty fostereth the growth of all things, and not every vain and feeble mind. Thus hath the wise Saná'í written:

> How can meagre reason comprehend
>   the Book,
> Or the spider trap a phoenix in its web?
> Wouldst thou that the mind not hold
>   thee in its snare?
> Seize it and enrol it in the school of
>   God instead!

16   On this plane, the traveller meeteth with many a trial and reverse. Now is he lifted up to heaven, now is he cast into the depths. As it hath been said: "Now Thou drawest me to the throne of the realms above, again Thou scorchest me in the fire of hell." The hidden mystery of this station is divulged in the following blessed verse from the Súrih of the Cave: "And thou mightest have seen the sun when it arose, pass on the right of their cave, and, when it set, leave them on the left, while they were in its spacious chamber. This is one of the signs of God. Guided indeed

is he whom God guideth; but for him whom He misleadeth, thou shalt by no means find a guardian and guide."[110]

If a soul could grasp the allusions that lie hid [17] in this single verse, it would suffice him. Such indeed are those whom He hath extolled as "men whom neither merchandise nor traffic beguile from the remembrance of God".[111]

This station is that of the true standard of [18] knowledge and the final end of tests and trials. Nor is it needed, in this realm, to seek after knowledge, for He hath said concerning the guidance of wayfarers on this plane, "Fear ye God; God will teach you",[112] and again, "Knowledge is a light which God casteth into the heart of whomsoever He willeth."[113]

Wherefore, one must make ready the receptacle [19] and become worthy of the descent of heavenly bestowals, that the all-sufficing Cup-Bearer may give one to drink of the wine of bounty from the crystal chalice of mercy. "For this let the striving strive!"[114] And now do I say, "Verily, we are God's, and to Him shall we return."[115]

If the lovers be among them that abide within [20] the precincts of THE ABODE OF THE LODESTONE OF HEARTS, no soul may dwell on this kingly throne save the countenance of love. I am powerless to describe this station or to depict it in words.

> Love shunneth this world and that world too;
> In him are lunacies seventy and two.
> The minstrel of love harpeth this lay:
> Servitude enslaveth, lordship doth betray.[116]

21   This plane demandeth pure love and unalloyed affection. In describing these companions He saith: "They speak not till He hath spoken, and act according to His commandment."[117]

22   In this station, neither the reign of the intellect is sufficient nor the rule of self. Thus one of the Prophets of God asked, "O my Lord, how shall I reach Thee?" And the answer came: "Leave thy self behind, and then approach Me."

23   In the estimation of such souls, to be seated amidst the sandals by the door is the same as to abide at the place of honour, and in the path of the Beloved the retreats of earthly beauty differ not from the field of a battle waged.

24   The dwellers of this abode know not the destination, yet they spur on their chargers. They see naught in the Beloved but His very Self. They find all words of sense to be meaningless, and

senseless words to be full of meaning. They cannot distinguish head from foot or one limb from another. To them the mirage is water itself and departure is the mystery of return. Wherefore hath it been said:

> The story of Thy beauty reached the
>   hermit's dell;
> Crazed, he sought the Tavern where the
>   wine they buy and sell.
> The love of Thee hath levelled down the
>   fort of patience;
> The pain of Thee hath firmly barred the
>   gate of hope as well.[118]

In this station, both instruction and appren-   25
ticeship are assuredly of no avail:

> The lovers' teacher is the Loved One's beauty,
> His face their lesson and their only book.
> Learning of wonderment, of longing love
>   their duty;
> Not on learned chapters and dull themes
>   they look.
> The chains that bind them are His musky
>   hair;

The Cyclic Scheme, to them, is but to Him
a stair.[119]

26   Here followeth a supplication to God—blessed
and glorified be He:

O Lord, O Thou Whose grace fulfilleth
every need!
To mention aught before Thee would be
sin indeed.
Allow this mote of knowledge hidden in
my soul
To free itself of lowly clay and reach its goal.
And grant this drop of wisdom that Thou
gavest me
To be at last united with Thy mighty sea.[120]

27   Thus do I say: There is no power nor strength
except in God, the Help in Peril, the Self-
Subsisting.

28   If the mystic knowers be among them that have
attained THE BEAUTY OF THE BELOVED, this station
is the throne of the inmost heart and the secret
of divine guidance. This is the seat of the mystery
"He doeth what He willeth, and ordaineth what
He pleaseth." Should all that are in heaven and on

earth attempt to unravel this exalted allusion and subtle mystery, from now until the Day whereon the Trumpet shall sound, yet would they fail to comprehend even a letter thereof, for this is the station of God's immutable decree and His fore-ordained mystery. Hence, when asked regarding this matter, He made reply: "It is a bottomless sea that none shall ever fathom." And when the question was repeated, He answered: "It is the blackest of nights through which none can find his way."[121]

Whoso comprehendeth this station will assur- 29 edly conceal it, and were he to reveal but the faintest trace thereof, they would assuredly hang him from the gallows. And yet, by God, were a true seeker to be found, I would divulge it to him; for He saith: "Love is a distinction never conferred upon a heart possessed by fear and dread."[122]

In truth, the wayfarer who journeyeth unto 30 God, who treadeth the snow-white Path and turneth towards the Crimson Pillar, will never reach his heavenly home unless his hands are empty of such worldly things as are cherished by men. "And he that feareth not God, God shall make him to fear all things; whereas all things fear him who feareth God."

Speak the Persian tongue, though the
    Arabian pleaseth more:
Love indeed doth have a hundred other
    tongues in store.[123]

31   How sweet in this connection is the following couplet:

Our hearts will be as open shells
Should He the pearls of grace bestow;
Our lives will ready targets be
Were He to hurl the darts of woe.

32   And were it not contrary to the commandment of the Book, I would surely have bestowed a part of My possessions upon My would-be murderer, and given him to inherit Mine earthly goods, and rendered him a myriad thanks, and solaced Mine own eyes with the touch of his hand. But what can I do? Neither have I any wealth, nor hath the Lord of destiny so decreed.

33   Methinks at this moment I perceive the musk-scented fragrance of the garment of Há' from the Joseph of Bahá; verily He seemeth near at hand, though ye may think Him far away.[124]

My soul doth sense the fragrant breath
Of a well-beloved soul:
The fragrance of that kindly friend
Who's my heart's desire and goal.

The duty of long years of love obey,
And tell the tale of blissful days gone by,
That land and sky may laugh aloud today,
And it may gladden mind and heart
    and eye.[125]

This is the realm of pure awareness and utter   34
self-effacement. Not even love can find a way to
this plane, nor doth affection have a place therein.
Wherefore is it said: "Love is a veil betwixt the
lover and the beloved." Here love becometh but
an obstructing veil, and aught save the Friend but
a curtain. Thus the wise Saná'í hath written:

None may approach that well-belov'd
Who harboreth his own desire;
None may embrace that beauteous form
Who's burdened with his own attire.

For this is the realm of God and is sanctified above
every allusion of His creatures.

35   Abiding in the court of rapture, the dwellers of this mansion wield with utmost joy and gladness the sceptres of divinity and lordship; and, established upon the lofty seats of justice, they exert their rule and bestow upon every soul its due. Those who drink of this cup abide beneath the canopy of glory, above the throne of the Ancient of Days, and dwell upon the seat of grandeur beneath the tabernacle of majesty. These are they that "know neither sun nor piercing cold".[126]

36   On this plane the highest heavens are neither opposed to, nor distinguished from, the lowly earth, for this is the realm of divine favours, not the arena of worldly contraries. Albeit at every moment a new condition be displayed, yet that condition is ever the same. Wherefore He saith in one instance, "Nothing whatsoever keepeth Him from being occupied with any other thing."[127] And in another He saith, "Verily, His ways differ every day."[128]

37   This is the food whose savour changeth not and whose colour altereth not. Wert thou to partake thereof, thou wouldst assuredly recite the verse "I have turned my face to Him Who hath created the heavens and the earth, following the right religion and submissive before God. I am not one

of those who add gods to God."[129] "And thus did We show Abraham the kingdom of the heavens and of the earth, that he might be stablished in knowledge."[130] Wherefore, put thy hand into thy bosom, then stretch it forth with power, and behold, thou shalt find it a light unto all the world.

How clear this crystal water that the enraptured Cup-Bearer passeth round! How exquisite this pure wine that the intoxicated Beauty doth proffer! How pleasing this draught of joy that floweth from the Heavenly Cup! Well is it with him who drinketh thereof, and tasteth of its sweetness, and attaineth unto its knowledge.   38

> No more than this will I impart to thee:
> The riverbed can never hold the sea.[131]

For its mystery lieth hid in the storehouses   39
of His inviolable protection and is laid up in the treasuries of His power. It is exalted above the highest essence of utterance and sanctified beyond the subtlest mode of explanation.

Astonishment here is highly prized, and utter   40
poverty greatly cherished. Wherefore hath He said, "Poverty is My pride."[132] And again: "God hath a people beneath the canopy of grandeur,

whom He hath concealed in the garment of poverty to exalt in rank."[133] These are they who see with His eyes and hear with His ears, as hath been recorded in the well-known tradition.[134]

41   Concerning this realm there is many a tradition and many a verse, whether of general or specific import, but two of these will suffice, that they may serve as a light for knowing hearts and bring delight to longing souls.

42   The first is His statement "O My servant! Obey Me, that I may make thee like unto Myself. For I say 'Be', and it is, and thou shalt say 'Be', and it shall be." And the second: "O son of Adam! Seek fellowship with none until thou hast found Me, and whensoever thou shalt long for Me, thou shalt find Me nigh unto thee."

43   Whatever high proofs and wondrous allusions are recounted herein concern but a single letter and a single point. For such is God's method, and no change canst thou find in His mode of dealing.[135]

44   I undertook to write this epistle some time ago in thy remembrance, and, since thy letter had not reached Me yet, I began with a few words of grievance and reproach. Now, thy new missive hath dispelled that feeling and hath caused Me

to send thee this letter. To speak of My love for thine eminence is needless. "Sufficient witness is God unto us."[136]

As for his eminence <u>Sh</u>aykh Muḥammad—may God, the Exalted, bless him!—I shall confine Myself to the two following lines, which I request be delivered to him: 45

> I seek thy nearness, more desired than
>   heaven in mine eyes;
> I see thy visage, fairer than the bowers
>   of Paradise.

When I entrusted this message of love to My pen, it refused the burden and swooned away. Then, coming to itself, it spoke and said, "Glory be to Thee! To Thee do I turn in penitence, and I am the first of them that implore Thy pardon."[137] All praise be to God, the Lord of the worlds!   46

> Let us tell, some other day
> This parting hurt and woe;
> Let us write, some other way,
> Love's secrets—better so.
> Leave blood and noise and all of these,
> And say no more of <u>Sh</u>ams-i-Tabríz.[138]

Peace be upon thee, and upon them who circle round thee and attain thy presence.

47   That which I had written ere this hath been eaten by the flies, so rich was the ink to their taste, even as Sa'dí hath said:

> I write no more, beleaguered by the flies
> That my sweet words have drawn about
>   the page.

48   And now the hand can write no more, and pleadeth that this is enough. Wherefore do I say: Far from the glory of my Lord, the All-Glorious, be that which His creatures affirm of Him!

Notes

1 *Epistle to the Son of the Wolf* (trans. Shoghi Effendi, Wilmette, IL: Bahá'í Publishing Trust, 1988), p. 15.

2 *Epistle to the Son of the Wolf*, p. 22.

3 *God Passes By* (Wilmette, IL: Bahá'í Publishing Trust, 1974, 2018 printing), pp. 192–93.

4 *God Passes By*, p. 216.

5 *God Passes By*, pp. 217 and 220.

6 From a previously untranslated Tablet.

7 Bahá'u'lláh, *Gleanings from the Writings of Bahá'u'lláh,* CLI, ¶2.

8 "*'Amá'* is defined as an extremely thin and subtle cloud, seen and then not seen. For shouldst thou gaze with the utmost care, thou wouldst discern something, but as soon as thou dost look again, it ceaseth to be seen. For this reason, in the usage of mystics who seek after truth, *'Amá'* signifieth the Universal Reality without individuations as such, for these individuations exist in the mode of uncompounded simplicity and oneness and are not differentiated from the Divine Essence. Thus they are individuated and not individuated. This is the station alluded to by the terms *Aḥadíyyih* [Absolute Oneness] and *'Amá'*. This is the station of the "Hidden Treasure"

mentioned in the Ḥadíth. The divine attributes, therefore, are individuations that exist in the Essence but are not differentiated therefrom. They are seen and then not seen. This, in brief, is what is meant by *'Amá'*." (From a previously untranslated Tablet of 'Abdu'l-Bahá.)

9 The Manifestation of God.

10 Qur'án 6:103.

11 Aḥmad, Muḥammad, and Maḥmúd are names and titles of the Prophet derived from the verb "to praise", "to extol".

12 Qur'án 17:110.

13 Cf. Qur'án 76:1.

14 Literally, "in the garden of Ghawthíyyih". The *Risáliy-i-Ghawthíyyih* is a mystical treatise by 'Abdu'l-Qádir-i-Gílání (ca. 1077–1166). The sentence that follows is a quotation from this work.

15 Qur'án 2:282, 16:69.

16 Qur'án 20:47.

17 'Aṭṭár (ca. 1119–1230) in his *Manṭiqu'ṭ-Ṭayr* (*The Conference of the Birds*) has elaborated seven valleys through which the birds pass in search of their king. Bahá'u'lláh refers to 'Aṭṭár's scheme of the valleys. Rúmí (1207–1273) alludes to the "seven cities of love" crossed by 'Aṭṭár.

18 Qur'án 29:69.

19 *Majnún* means "madman". This is the title of the celebrated lover of ancient Persian and Arabian lore whose beloved was Laylí. Symbolizing true human love bordering on the divine, the story has been

the theme of many Persian romantic poems, most famously that of Niẓámí, written in 1188.

20 Arabic proverb.

21 A reference to the Islamic profession of faith: "No God is there but God, and Muḥammad is the Messenger of God."

22 Saná'í (ca. 1045–1131).

23 Saná'í.

24 Qur'án 50:30.

25 Rúmí.

26 An allusion to the Ḥadíth in which God is said to address the Prophet Muḥammad in these words: "But for Thee, I would not have created the spheres."

27 From a poem of Bahá'u'lláh.

28 Hátif-i-Iṣfahání (d.1783).

29 Qur'án 67:3.

30 Qur'án 41:53.

32 From a Ḥadíth.

32 Shaykh Abú Ismá'íl 'Abdu'lláh Anṣárí of Hirát (1006–1089), a Ṣúfí master, poet, and scholar.

33 Qur'án 1:6.

34 Rúmí.

35 Qur'án 2:156.

36 Qur'án 4:78.

37 Qur'án 18:39.

38 The Prophet Muḥammad.

39 Rúmí.

40 Qur'án 16:61.

41 From a Ḥadíth.

42 From a Ḥadíth.

43 Qur'án 83:28.
44 From a Ḥadíth.
45 From a prayer of Imám ʻAlí.
46 "But for Thee" refers to the Ḥadíth quoted in note 26. "We have failed to know Thee" alludes to a prayer attributed to Muḥammad that says, "We have not known Thee, O God, as Thou oughtest to be known." "Or even closer" alludes to Qur'án 53:9.
47 Saʻdí (ca. 1213–1292), author of the *Gulistán* and other poetical works.
48 From a Ḥadíth.
49 Rúmí; a reference to Qur'án 18:71.
50 Qur'án 57:3.
51 Rúmí.
52 This refers to Baháʼuʼlláh Himself, Who had not yet declared His mission.
53 Qur'án 4:130.
54 Cf. ʻAṭṭár.
55 Ibn-i-Fáriḍ (1181–1235).
56 From a Ḥadíth.
57 Cf. Qur'án 50:22.
58 Saná'í.
59 The Prophet Muḥammad.
60 From a Ḥadíth.
61 Rúmí.
62 Qur'án 9:51.
63 Rúmí.
64 Qur'án 76:5.
65 From a Ḥadíth.
66 Qur'án 28:88.

67 Qur'án 15:21.

68 Hátif-i-Iṣfahání.

69 From a Ḥadíth.

70 Attributed to Rúmí.

71 A reference to two Ṣúfí concepts. The doctrine of the unity of existence is commonly ascribed to Ibnu'l-'Arabí (1165–1240), that of the unity of appearance to Aḥmad Sirhindí (1564–1624). See 'Abdu'l-Bahá, *Some Answered Questions,* chapter 82.

72 Qur'án 17:79. A reference to the station of the Manifestation of God.

73 "The word 'Guardian' in the Seven Valleys has no connection with the Bahá'í Guardianship." (From a letter dated 8 January 1949 written on behalf of Shoghi Effendi.)

74 Qur'án 2:90.

75 Rúmí.

76 Ibn-i-Fáriḍ.

77 In what follows, Bahá'u'lláh interprets the meaning of each of the five letters comprising the word "sparrow" (*gunjishk*) in Persian.

78 The recipient of this Tablet was Mírzá Hádí Qazvíní.

79 Allusions to the Muslim profession of faith. See note 21.

80 The Báb.

81 An allusion to Bahá'u'lláh's approaching declaration.

82 From a Ḥadíth.

83 Rúmí.

84 Qur'án 76:5.

85 Qur'án 21:69.

[86] Qur'án 67:3.

[87] Rúmí.

[88] Rúmí.

[89] Rúmí.

[90] Qur'án 4:78–79.

[91] A reference to the three levels of certitude in the Islamic mystical tradition.

[92] Qur'án 39:53.

[93] Cf. Qur'án 37:173.

[94] See note 71.

[95] Rúmí. Bahá'u'lláh is here comparing Shaykh 'Abdu'r-Raḥmán, the recipient of the Tablet, with Ḥusámu'd-Dín Chalabí, to whom Rúmí dedicated his *Mathnaví*. Ḥusámu'd-Dín means "sword of faith".

[96] Sa'dí.

[97] Qur'án 41:30.

[98] Qur'án 11:112.

[99] Sa'dí.

[100] Sa'dí.

[101] Rúmí.

[102] From a prayer attributed to Imám 'Alí.

[103] Cf. Rúmí. Here Rúmí tells a story of four evil birds which, when put to death, changed into four birds of goodness. The allegory refers to subduing evil qualities and replacing them with good.

[104] Qur'án 89: 29–30.

[105] Cf. Qur'án 41:53.

[106] Qur'án 17:14.

[107] Famed writers on grammar and rhetoric.

[108] Rúmí.

[109] Qur'án 59:19.
[110] Qur'án 18:17.
[111] Qur'án 24:37.
[112] Qur'án 2:282.
[113] From a Ḥadíth.
[114] Qur'án 83:26.
[115] Qur'án 2:156.
[116] Rúmí.
[117] Qur'án 21:27.
[118] Sa'dí.
[119] Rúmí. A reference to the Cyclic Theory of Avicenna (Abu-'Alí Síná [980–1037]).
[120] Rúmí.
[121] From a Ḥadíth.
[122] From a Ḥadíth.
[123] Rúmí.
[124] An intimation of Bahá'u'lláh's imminent Manifestation.
[125] Rúmí.
[126] Qur'án 76:13.
[127] A famous adage cited in many Islamic sources.
[128] Qur'án 55:29.
[129] Cf. Qur'án 6:79.
[130] Qur'án 6:75.
[131] Rúmí.
[132] From a Ḥadíth.
[133] From a Ḥadíth.
[134] See the Seven Valleys, ¶44.
[135] Cf. Qur'án 35:43, 48:23.
[136] Qur'án 4:166.
[137] Cf. Qur'án 7:143.

[138] Rúmí. <u>Sh</u>ams–i–Tabríz was the Ṣúfí who exerted a powerful influence on Rúmí, diverting his attention from science to mysticism. A great part of Rúmí's works are dedicated to him.